TRUTHS THAT CHANGE US INSIDE

MARK FINLEY and
STEVEN MOSLEY

Pacific Press® Publishing Association
Nampa, Idaho
Oshawa, Ontario, Canada

Edited by B. Russell Holt
Cover design by Tim Larson
Cover photo by Romilly Lockyer © Image Bank

Copyright © 2000 by
Pacific Press® Publishing Association
Printed in the United States of America
All Rights Reserved

Unless otherwise indicated, Scripture quotations are from
the New King James version.

ISBN 0-8163-1814-X

01 02 03 04 • 5 4 3 2

Contents

Introduction

There are some things in life that matter. They count. They make a dramatic difference. The things that really matter in life are those eternal truths that change us inside.

The Bible characters in both the Old and New Testaments discovered these eternal, life-changing truths. When David discovered one of these life-changing truths, he cried out, "Create in me a new heart, O God" (Psalm 51:10). When Joseph discovered one of these life-changing truths as he was being seduced by Potiphar's wife, he cried out, "How then can I do this great wickedness, and sin against God?" (Genesis 39:9). When Job discovered one of these life-changing truths, he cried out, "Though He slay me yet will I trust Him" (Job 13:15). When the apostle Paul discovered one of these life-changing truths, he cried out, "I have fought a good fight, I have finished the race, I have kept the faith. Finally, there is laid up for me the crown of righteousness, which the Lord, the righteous Judge, shall give me in that Day, and not to me only but also to all who have loved His appearing" (2 Timothy 4:7).

Each of these Bible characters discovered a truth that made a dramatic difference. David discovered the truth of forgiveness. Joseph discovered the truth of moral purity found in God's law. Job discovered the real truth about life after death. And Paul discovered the truth of the second coming of our Lord.

Scripture is full of these truths. They are eternal. They are changeless, and they are timeless. But these truths are not isolated dogmas. They are living, renewing, vitalizing principles which radically make us over inside. As you read these pages, I pray that you will discover these eternal, transforming truths—truths that truly change us inside—and that your life will be enriched and renewed. May the Lord of all truth impart His power to your life as you read these pages.

Mark Finley

Open Hearts
Heal

A certain wit once observed, "Any time you think you have influence, try ordering someone else's dog around."

It doesn't work too well, does it?

All of us have emotions and behaviors in our lives that sometimes act just like someone else's dog. We just can't get a handle on them; we can't control them. We may feel that we have some influence—in the workplace or at home—but when it comes to these habits, we feel pretty helpless. Most people struggle with some habits in their life, some kind of compulsion that gets the best of them, some pesky little beast inside that just won't get house-trained.

Maybe it's chronic anxiety. You just can't stop worrying over the smallest things.

Maybe it's an inability to set boundaries. You just can't seem to say "no" when you need to. On the other hand, maybe it's a need to control other people. You feel compelled to make others get in shape—your shape.

Maybe it's a habit of falling for the wrong kind of people.

Maybe it's overeating.

Maybe it's criticism, gossip. Maybe it's an addiction to sex or alcohol.

As human beings, we struggle with that thing inside us that acts like someone else's dog.And, of course, a lot has been written about the problem. Bookstores are full of self-help best sellers with all kinds of theories about how to deal with problem behavior, all kinds of principles and programs and steps.

So, in this book, we've decided to ask a basic question: "Are there biblical principles which work?"

We wanted to find out what really produces change, what really helps people grow. So we went for answers to people who are on the front lines—Christian counselors and pastors who face these issues all the time. What do they say to individuals who come to them for help? And what principles have made the biggest difference in people's lives?

As a result, we've been able to zero in on the truths that really do help people break bad habits. And that's what we're going to be discussing in this book—principles that get to the root of our problems, "how-to's" that move people to a healthier place.

In this chapter, we'll look at the first important truth. In talking with Christian counselors, we've discovered very quickly that there is one obstacle that keeps many people from getting on the road to growth and recovery.

Bob Oltoff: "Fear is one of the big motivators that happens inside for all of us. And to face our feelings, means that we are vulnerable. So we want to move to a place of self-protection where we can feel safe and secure and in control rather than open up to our feelings and feel vulnerable. We're afraid; we don't know what's going to happen."

David Coe: "I grew up an abused and beaten child. My Dad would just . . . well, he beat me into unconsciousness a number of times. So, as a result of all that, a great deal of anger and pain has built up. Growing up knowing that you aren't loved creates an extreme amount of pain, and as a result of that pain, you hate too. And the hate causes guilt. So it's unending, almost a whirlwind, that you're caught up in. Then, when you have to put up a front for all that and keep all that in check, it's an unbelievable pressure."

Keeping the problem a secret. Keeping the problem hidden. That's one of the biggest obstacles to change. A closed heart can't heal. A closed heart can't grow. This book, *Truths That Change Us Inside*, can help you start opening up, start becoming more honest—with yourself, with others, and most of all, with God. In these pages, you'll discover the fundamental principles that make the greatest difference.So, let's look at an alternative to the nice façade so many of us wear on the outside of our lives. Interestingly enough, we find this alternative in the Psalms of the Old Testament. Did you know that many of these psalms provide a model for us—an example—of how we can break through, how we can be more real? There is a distinct language, which we may trace throughout the book of Psalms, a tone and a cadence that suggests a child coming before a parent and pouring it all out. The Psalms cry out for help. Forty-one of them are dominated by pleas for rescue. The verses tumble out directly and simply: "Help me; I'm in trouble." We see people appealing to God, often desperately, in all kinds of situations.

There's a reason for the forty-one urgent appeals recorded in the Psalms; it's a very basic lesson that sometimes slips by us. God is simply telling us: "It's OK to pour your heart out to Me." We can come to Him as freely as a child running to a parent. We may not always ask for the right things; God will certainly not always answer us in the way we want Him to. But He does invite us to come. We have the privilege of using the innocent, spontaneous language of children who are secure in their parents' unconditional acceptance.

Before we are anything else, we are needy children, totally dependent on our parents. That is true at the beginning of physical life, and it's true also, at the beginning of spiritual life. It's also true at the start of every day of our Christian life. God invites us to open ourselves to Him, to share our joys and sorrows, our pain and our disappointment and even our weaknesses and our failings. It's good to know the language of "help" or "I'm in trouble." The Psalms show us that it's good to be secure enough to come and plead at the feet of our heavenly Father who cherishes us.

Paul Coneff: "In Psalm 109, David is very angry about people who have hurt him. He goes on and on, and he's very, very angry. Then finally he sees that his anger is eating him alive. So he asks God for mercy. And then he says, 'Lord, deal with me . . . my heart is wounded within me.' So he has gone from his external anger to taking responsibility for his negative reaction to the people that have hurt him. He's saying, 'My heart is wounded within me.' He's gone from the external anger to the internal pain. And then he ends up saying, 'Praise God in His sanctuary.' We don't know if the people who had hurt him changed, but we do know that David found peace and healing and freedom because he was able to be honest with God about the feelings inside of him."

Honesty can be a powerful force in your life. Openness can be a powerful force. That's the first principle you have to understand if you are ever to experience meaningful change. A closed heart stays wounded. Only an open heart can heal.

Deane Wolcott: "Many people feel they have to be in control, that they have to be strong, and that being strong means you don't show any weakness or vulnerability or need. In reality, however, the greatest strength comes from sharing with other people—sharing your real needs, your real concerns, your real vulnerabilities. I often see people who have kind of separated from each other in relationships when they face a major problem such as cancer. And I see all of the additional stress that both partners face in a relationship. It's wonderful, when people learn they can share openly about their real concerns and fears, to see how they're both actually strengthened by that process of sharing."

We need to be open before God. And we need to be open before others who are trustworthy. That's important. Did you know that the apostle Paul emphasized this very point of openness? He appealed for this kind of honesty between believers. Listen to what he told the Corinthian Christians in 2 Corinthians 6:11, 13. He's writing to a group that was plagued by very serious problems including lawsuits and incest. He says, "We have spoken freely to you, Corinthians, and opened wide our hearts to you. As a fair exchange—I speak as to my children—open wide your hearts also" (NIV).

Open wide your hearts. When we first open up our hearts to God, an inner healing process begins. He floods our lives with mercy and forgiveness. When we share our lives with a trusted Christian friend, healing begins. Why? Because only an open heart can heal. That's a foundational principle in Scripture that Christian counselors have discovered is vital to change. You can't keep pretending. You can't keep problems a secret. You can't bury them deep enough. If you do, you'll remain stuck in your problems.

Friends, something wonderful, something liberating happens when we finally become transparent.

Marilyn Brown: "I grew up in an environment in which we didn't talk about our problems. We were very religious, and we went to church often, and we always wore our Sunday best. After I got divorced, I joined a recovery group because I wanted to deal with issues in my life. For the first time, I heard people telling the truth about their flaws, about the struggles they had. I was amazed that they could be so open. Eventually I learned to do that, and it was so freeing to tell the truth about myself out loud—to myself and to other people."

Opening up to God and another Christian friend can be such a powerful experience, such a liberating experience.

Friends, God wants very much to deal with the root of our problems. God wants to heal us on the inside. That's one reason He gives us His Word. In Hebrews 4:12 we find God sharing with us how to transform our lives from the inside. He says, "For the word of God is living and powerful, and sharper than any two-edged sword, piercing even to the division of soul and spirit, and of joints and marrow, and is a discerner of the thoughts and intents of the heart." God designed His Word to go deep. He is the One who searches minds and hearts. He wants His Word to unlock our secrets, to touch our hurts, to expose our blind spots. So we need to open ourselves up to that instrument in our lives. We need to let God do His work.

God promises healing when we become transparent. God promises to give us something precious when we open ourselves up. Let me give you one specific example. This is what He promises to those afflicted by worry, those burdened by chronic anxiety. It's recorded in Philippians 4:6, 7. "Be anxious for nothing, but in everything by prayer and supplication, with thanksgiving, let your request be made known to God; and the peace of God, which surpasses all understanding, will guard your hearts and minds through Christ Jesus."

God says, "Pour everything out in prayer. Let your requests be known, your hopes be known, your fears be known. When you take a risk, when you become vulnerable, I will give you something precious." What is it? The peace of God. It's something that surpasses understanding. It's something that can guard our hearts and minds.

God always gives us far more than we give Him. God always fills us when we open ourselves, when we empty ourselves before Him.

Now, let me tell you about a very important part of honesty. Honesty involves owning up. Honesty involves accepting responsibility for our actions. We're not responsible for the bad things done to us. We're not responsible for what we didn't get in our childhood. But we *are* responsible for our present, for our present responses. We can't pretend that it's all someone else's fault. We can't pretend that our problems will disappear if certain other people disappear or if we simply move to another place or if we get another job, or if we join another church. We have to acknowledge that our emotions and our behavior are *our* responsibility, no one else's.

The Bible clearly tells us that confessing our sins to God—owning up to them before Him—is important. It also tells us about owning up before others. "Confess your trespasses to one another, and pray for one another, that you may be healed" (James 5:16). It's important to be honest when we've hurt another person. It's important to be honest about our failings. James indicates that that's part of the healing process.

Frederick II, King of Prussia, was inspecting a prison in Berlin one day. One after another, the prisoners vigorously protested their innocence. Each claimed to have been wrongfully accused. Only one prisoner remained silent. So Frederick asked him, "You, there! Why are you here?"

"Armed robbery, your Majesty."

"Are you guilty?"

"Yes, indeed. I deserve my punishment."

The king summoned the warden. "Guard," he commanded, "release this guilty wretch at once. I'll not have him in this prison corrupting all these fine, innocent people here."

Accepting responsibility for our behavior is the first step toward freedom. It's an essential part of the honesty that heals.

Paul Coneff: "I've found that those people who are usually going to find healing are those that are able to take responsibility either for the mistakes they've made or the way they've reacted to other people who have hurt them. As long as they're blaming others and it's somebody else's problem, they don't usually find healing. I know, in my own life, when negative things happened to me as I was growing up, I tended to develop a negative attitude that was hurting me. And until I could take responsibility for how I was reacting in a negative way, then I wasn't able to get healing. I wasn't able to experience freedom."

Do you know what happens when we become honest before God and others? Do you know what happens when we accept responsibility for our own lives?

We start to experience love and forgiveness. You might fear the opposite is true. You might fear that you'll be accepted, you'll be loved, only as long as you keep things hidden. But those secret things are precisely what prevent you from truly receiving grace and love. They set up a barrier. They create a wall between you and God and between you and other people, as well.

Honest confession. Honest sharing. These are the things that open the way to forgiveness and love. Paul made this clear to the church in Corinth. The Corinthian believers were plagued by serious problems. They had plenty to hide. But Paul asked them to open up, to confront their weaknesses. And then he told them, "I do not say this to condemn; for I have said before that you are in our hearts, to die together and to live together" (2 Corinthians 7:3).

"You are in our hearts, to die together and to live

together." What a beautiful expression of grace! That's what real love is like. It comes to weak, sinful people. It comes to people who don't deserve it. It comes to people who have hurt others and who are hurting. But it *doesn't* come to people who keep their hearts closed. It *doesn't* come to people who close themselves up around secrets. Love comes when we're honest. Love comes when we're real. Love comes when we risk being vulnerable.

Marilyn Brown: "I was going through a pretty wild time in my life when I joined that recovery group. I was acting out, and I was doing things I knew were wrong. I talked about it there, and I shared my struggles. They understood. They understood why I was doing what I was doing. They listened; they could relate to my struggles. And they loved me anyway. That was really powerful for me. It was really incredible to have people love me when I didn't feel that I deserved to be loved, that I had earned it. I wasn't being good, and I was compelled to love God more because of that. I was kind of overwhelmed. I felt like my heart grew, that I loved other people more. That became part of a whole born-again experience for me."

Friends, a closed heart keeps hurting. An open heart heals. We need to drop the façade. We need to stop playing games. We need to become honest before God and others. There's great power in that, power for real change.

There's power in opening our hearts.

There's power in accepting responsibility for where we are.

There's power in confessing our sins and our mistakes.

There's power in sharing ourselves honestly with trustworthy people.

David Coe: "Once I was in treatment and began to deal with the things in my life—once I found acceptance from the others that were there, as well—it was almost like a storm being calmed. I finally realized that I didn't have to put the mask on and let people see only what I wanted them to see. I could be myself. And so, yes, there's great relief in that. There's great comfort in that."

The writer of the book of Hebrews shows us the end result of this kind of honesty. There's a wonderful passage in which he is talking about what it means to have Jesus Christ as our High Priest, our Advocate. This is a High Priest we can confide in, One we can confess to. This is a High Priest who represents us before the Holy Father in heaven. Having such a High Priest then, brings this result: "Let us draw near with a true heart in full assurance of faith, having our hearts sprinkled from an evil conscience" (Hebrews 10:22).

We can draw near. We can draw near with a true heart, an honest heart. We can draw near in full assurance. Why? Because being transparent before God allows Him to get into our hearts. It allows Him to cleanse us. It allows Him to take care of our guilty conscience. It allows Him to take care of our hurts. It allows Him to pour His grace and love inside of us.

Do you want to draw near to Jesus Christ today, right now? Do you want to take the first step on the road to wholeness and healing and recovery? I invite you to take a risk. I invite you to become vulnerable. Make a decision about the things you've kept hidden. Do something about the fear that keeps you from revealing yourself.

Open your heart to God right now. Tell Him all about it. Tell Him why you're hurting. Tell Him why you're angry. Tell Him everything. And resolve to find people you can trust, people you can share with honestly.

Will you do that? Please don't hold back. Please don't hang on to things that put up barriers between yourself and others. Please give it all up in the name of Jesus Christ, as we pray.

"Dear Father, we need You. We need You inside of us. There are hurtful things in our hearts right now. There are ugly things in our hearts. We lay them all before You. Please help us to be open and transparent. Please give us the strength to trust You in this way. We ask for Your forgiveness and love. We open our hearts so that You can fill us. Thank You for responding. Thank You for being generous. In the name of Your beloved Son. Amen."

The Cross Absorbs Our Hurt

People sometimes get stuck doing things over and over that they really want to stop. They feel regret. They feel remorse. But they seem compelled to go on and on. And they often don't realize that the substance they abuse or the behavior they indulge in is really a kind of anesthetic. They're trying to feel less. In this chapter, we'll learn about a dramatic alternative to the cycle of addiction— in a most unlikely place. And we'll discover a solution in the One who felt so much for us.

A young man named Don was having the time of his life. At least that's what it looked like on the outside. He'd been going out with quite a string of attractive girl-friends. Other men looked at him enviously. But inside, Don was miserable. He was falling apart. His dating had become something compulsive. He found himself using one woman after another just to get out of his own depression. When he felt down, he had to have some female reassurance.

Don knew he wasn't being fair with his partners. He'd been raised in a very strict home. Often he repented and promised God to change his ways. But the pattern continued. Finally, Don went to see a Christian counselor who used spiritual, biblical principles in his work. Don just wanted to change the vicious cycle of his behavior. He just wanted a formula to change his destructive habits. But slowly, this young man realized that there was a reason he had these serious bouts of depression. There was a reason he was compelled to use women the way he did.

Behind Don's depression was an emptiness, an inability to absorb love in a healthy way. And so he was compelled, over and over, to try to get love in unhealthy ways. Don wasn't able to get a handle on his destructive behavior until he faced the brokenness inside, until he began to understand what God's unconditional love is all about, what grace is all about. It was only when that really sank in that he could have healthier relationships with women.

Christian counselors have been discovering something important about addictions, all kinds of addictions. They have found that behind addiction, there is always brokenness, always pain, always emptiness, always some void. And if a person doesn't deal with the inner problem, he or she can never really get a handle on the behavior.

Paul Coneff: "I work with people that are dealing with addictions. A lot of times I find that behind the addiction, let's say it's alcohol, they're covering up emotional pain, and the alcohol numbs it. Food can also numb that pain. Pornography can numb the pain of loneliness or some other pain. So I've found that behind the particular addiction a person may have—when we get behind the anger, when we get behind the thing that's driving them, the thing they end up being addicted to—often there's emotional pain that is negative. And the addiction is just a way to numb that and avoid that."

Behind the addictions that chain us and behind the compulsions that bind us and behind the sins that imprison us, there is brokenness. Behind problem behaviors, there is some issue that we're not dealing with.

So how *do* we deal with that brokenness deep inside of us? How *do* we find healing?

Let's look at an important principle related to how we heal the hurt inside. I'd like to share with you something the prophet Jeremiah wrote. This man endured a lot of anguish in his life; he felt very isolated; he endured a lot of rejection. The people of Israel were moving away from God. Idols were their particular anesthetic of choice. They numbed the emptiness inside with various heathen practices, many of them involving fertility rites.

In his book, Jeremiah spoke out about people proclaiming "Peace, peace," when there really was no peace. People were trying to say things were just fine, when actually they were rotting inside. Jeremiah warned the people that they were sliding away from God. Jeremiah felt their pain when they were numb to it. He said, "For the hurt of the daughter of my people I am hurt" (Jeremiah 8:21). And then he cried out, "Is there no balm in Gilead, is there no physician there? Why then is there no recovery for the health of the daughter of my people?" (Verse 22).

Jeremiah believed that there had to be a balm, there had to be something that would really heal his people. There had to be recovery. And his faith proved to be prophetic. His "balm in Gilead" pointed forward to the ministry of Jesus Christ in Galilee. Jesus became the Great Healer for His people.

But there's a *special* way that Jesus can become a Healer today. A special way in which He can heal those hurts that lie behind so many problem behaviors. A special way that He can heal that brokenness. The Bible talks about this special healing process, and it centers around the Cross—Christ's experience of crucifixion.

Now usually, when we think of the Cross, we think of Jesus dying for human sin. We think of atonement. And that is indeed what happened at the Cross. Jesus made salvation possible; He made forgiveness before God possible.

But something else also happened at the Cross—something that we may not have looked at carefully enough. Jesus died for our sins, but He also died for our suffering, our deepest hurts, our deepest pain. He died to heal us from our brokenness. He died to reconcile us to God. When the gap between us and God is breached, His grace flows into our lives, and healing occurs.

The writer of Hebrews discusses why Jesus became a man and why He suffered. And this is what he says: "But we see Jesus, who was made a little lower than the angels, for the suffering of death crowned with glory and honor, that He, by the grace of God, might taste death for everyone" (Hebrews 2:9).

Christ's incarnation ultimately resulted in glory and honor. It resulted in redemption. But the means of getting to that glory was not an easy one; it required the suffering of death. Jesus had to taste death for everyone. Now, Jesus did that in a legal sense to justify us before God. He took on the penalty of sin—death—as our Substitute. But I believe He also tasted death in another sense. He tasted the things that hurt us most deeply. He experienced our worst nightmares.

Paul Coneff: "When people come in for counseling, I have the privilege of sharing the Cross with them. I'll draw a cross on the board, and on one side I'll put down that He died for our sins; we all know that. Then I'll start walking them through the other side. I'll ask them, 'How did He feel when He was left alone by the disciples three times in Gethsemane? What did He feel when He was sold for thirty pieces of silver?' And they'll say, 'He felt betrayed.' After we get all these words up on the board, if they've been betrayed, they'll identify with Jesus being betrayed. If they've been humiliated or shamed, maybe through sexual abuse, they're going to identify with being stripped naked, having their physical boundaries violated, and being humiliated and shamed. If they feel rejected, they see that He was rejected too, and that taps into their sense of rejection. They see that Jesus died, not only for their sins, but for their suffering—and that gives Him the right to heal them."

Think about it for a moment. What did Jesus endure on the cross? He endured every kind of abuse. He was verbally abused by Roman soldiers and priests. He was mocked and spit on. He was physically abused in horrible ways. He experienced religious abuse. Authority figures from the temple were the loudest in their mockery. They were the ones most determined to destroy Him. He experienced rejection. He was rejected by the people He had come to save; rejected by the leaders of the day; rejected even by His closest friends.

But worst of all, He experienced God's rejection; He felt God turning away from Him as the embodiment of sin. That's what tore the Son of God apart.

And this is why Jesus Christ can touch our deepest hurts.

He's able to empathize. The writer of Hebrews puts it this way: "For in that He Himself has suffered, being tempted, He is able to aid those who are tempted" (Hebrews 2:18). This passage is talking about why Jesus can be our merciful and faithful High Priest, why He can intercede for us. The answer is that He suffered; He knows what we're going through. He knows the worst that we can go through, and He knows all about it. That's why He can come to our aid. He helps us not just to keep us from sinning. He helps us face the pain, to deal with the hurt, to heal the brokenness. He can do it. He has earned the right.

Paul Coneff: "I had somebody come into my office who had really experienced a lot of betrayal in his life. As we went through the experience of Jesus on the cross, it really touched him in the area of his betrayal. He saw that Jesus had been betrayed for him and as him. And because of that, he was able to open up and share his pain and his anger and his frustration with God. As we prayed for him, Jesus could bring healing and freedom and peace to this person because He had gone through betrayal and He had earned the right to bring healing."

Kim Delaura: "He identified Himself completely with me—meaning my emotions, my sins that He took on Himself when He hung there on the cross. And that brought me a great feeling of acceptance and also of safety and relief, knowing that He could identify with me and carry that on my behalf."

Do you have hurts deep inside? Do you have pain that you haven't been able to face? A pain that keeps driving you to do things you don't want to do? Is there some brokenness in your life? Please consider right now exactly what Jesus went through on your behalf. As you read the following selections from the Bible, consider how close Jesus can come to you as a Healer, as the wounded Healer:

Here's a picture from Psalm 22 of what Jesus suffered. It's a remarkable prophecy of what actually happened on the cross. "My God, My God, why have You forsaken Me? . . . But I am a worm, and no man; a reproach of men, and despised of the people. All those who see Me ridicule Me; they shoot out the lip, they shake the head, saying, 'He trusted in the Lord, let Him rescue Him; . . .' I am poured out like water, and all My bones are out of joint; My heart is like wax; it has melted within Me. My strength is dried up like a potsherd, and My tongue clings to My jaws; you have brought Me to the dust of death. For dogs have surrounded Me; the congregation of the wicked has enclosed Me. They pierced My hands and My feet; I can count all My bones. They look and stare at Me. They divide My garments among them, and for My clothing they cast lots." (Psalm 22:1,6-8,14-18).

The prophet Isaiah also pictures Christ's experience on the cross very vividly: "Surely He has borne our griefs and carried our sorrows; yet we esteemed Him stricken, smitten by God, and afflicted. But He was wounded for our transgressions, He was bruised for our iniquities; the chastisement for our peace was upon Him, and by His stripes we are healed" (Isaiah 53:4, 5).

Jesus on the cross brings us healing. He heals our brokenness. I don't think many of us have understood that part of the good news. We are healed by His stripes. He has carried our sorrows. He was chastised so we could experience peace.

Jesus took on human suffering on the cross. He took on our deepest hurts. And something happens, something miraculous happens, when people really understand this amazing truth. Yes, there is a balm in Gilead. There is a Physician there. There is recovery. And we find it at the cross of Christ. Listen to how Paul expresses it in Colossians 1:19, 20: "For it pleased the Father that in Him all the fullness should dwell, and by Him to reconcile all things to Himself, by Him, whether things on earth or things in heaven, having made peace through the blood of His cross."

God the Father reconciled all things to Himself through Jesus Christ, through that sacrificial act on the cross. So often, our deepest hurts alienate us from God. It's hard for us to picture a loving heavenly Father. So many times we're filled with anger and guilt and shame. We hold the bad things that happened to us against Him. But God in Christ says, "I understand; I've been there; I took it all on. I suffered all the abuse you suffered, and more."

God reconciles sinful human beings to Himself. And God also reconciles shameful secrets. God also reconciles mistreatment. God reconciles rejection and abandonment. God reconciles abuse. God reconciles words that have wounded us. God reconciles *all things!* Do you see it? *All things!* Nothing has happened to you that is not taken in by the Cross. Nothing has happened to you that is not surrounded by Christ's sacrificial love.

And what does Christ create as a result? What does He create through His shed blood?

Peace. He "made peace through the blood of His cross." Yes, indeed. We can finally find peace when we open up our deepest hurts to the wounded Healer, to the One who tasted death for us, the One who tasted suffering for us—and turned it into something redemptive.

Remember, behind addictions, behind problem behaviors, there lies some brokenness, something we want to numb, something we want to anesthetize. And we can't really deal with those behaviors unless we deal with the hurt, the pain, that is driving them.

Thank God that the Cross gives us a way to face that pain! It allows us to face the brokenness, but not be destroyed by it. The cross of Jesus Christ absorbs our deepest hurts. That's a truth that changes people. That's a truth that can transform your life.

But that truth has to sink in. It has to touch you in some way. It's not enough just to nod your head. It's not enough just to give mental assent. As Paul prayed, "May the Lord direct your hearts into the love of God" (2 Thessalonians 3:5). The sacrificial love of Christ has to sink into your heart. You have to face your pain in the light of the Cross. You have to see for yourself just how Christ's sufferings touch yours. And when you do that, something wonderful happens. You find great personal power in the Cross. You find healing—great healing.

David Coe: "I began to realize the huge impact on my life that God made when He sent Jesus. I realized that He gave everything, whereas my father gave nothing. It created a bond between God and me that had never happened before. The joy and the peace within the soul that this understanding creates is immeasurable. You are right with the world; you are right with God. You can then start to mend the fences with your families, and you can become right with them, as well. It changes everything."

Bob Oltoff: "A man came to see me who had been

raised in an alcoholic home. Another family in the neighborhood treated him with love. But unfortunately, this became a trap; three of the males in that family molested him. But he stayed within that family because he had more love there than he had in his own home. Later, he had problems with his wife regarding intimacy. And part of that was because of his own vulnerability and not being able to be open. He was in a mode of self-protection. As we talked, the power of Christ came in and healed those memory pictures that were going on inside him. All of a sudden, it opened him up to a whole new world of intimacy and truthfulness and transparency with God. And it had an incredible impact on his marriage."

What a marvelous Savior we have in Jesus Christ! His sacrifice on the cross goes deeper than we've imagined. It can touch us in ways that we have not yet fathomed. It brings us closer to God than we can ever imagine. Listen to the writer of Hebrews describing Christ's unique ministry as our High Priest in heaven. He is unique because He has tasted death for us—and yet continues forever as our Intercessor. "Therefore He is also able to save to the uttermost those who come to God through Him, since He always lives to make intercession for them" (Hebrews 7:25).

"Save to the uttermost." Do you realize what that means? Jesus dealt thoroughly with the sin problem. He paid the penalty of death for us. And He also suffered for us. This is the One who is presenting our case before the Father. This is the One who is making intercession for us. He understands. He's been there. He has felt everything that we have felt.

That's why we can come confidently to God, through

Christ. We are identified with Christ. All of our sin and anger and shame is absorbed in Him. We are identified with the Son of God. We are accepted, adopted into a heavenly family where love wipes away every tear, wipes away all the abuse.

Listen to Paul's wonderful affirmation: "And because you are sons, God has sent forth the Spirit of His Son into your hearts, crying out, 'Abba, Father!' Therefore you are no longer a slave but a son" (Galatians 4:6, 7). God makes us sons and daughters—not just in theory, but in our hearts. He sends His Spirit into our hearts to affirm that. Once, we heard old hurtful voices echoing in there. We felt old shaming acts echoing still. We kept rehearsing those hurts over and over. But now a voice calls out, "Abba! Daddy!" Now we can know that we are fully accepted, that we're unconditionally loved. We can walk straight into the arms of a heavenly Father.

We're no longer slaves to those old disappointments and hurts; we're no longer bound by them. We have the freedom of sons and daughters. God lavishes His love on us. We are cherished in the beloved Son of God.

Friend, the cross of Christ absorbs our deepest hurts. Have you experienced that? Have you gone there to find healing? There is a balm in Gilead. There is a Physician there. Please come to Him right now. Please don't let another day go by with that pain inside that keeps driving you. Please don't let those destructive habits keep tying you up.

Please come to the Cross and find healing. By His stripes you can be healed. By His chastisement you can find peace, right now.

Tell Yourself
the Truth

Man: "I was waiting, like, ten minutes! What is the matter with you? I think you missed the exit on purpose. You're trying to humiliate me. What do you think I looked like, standing there like an idiot in the lobby. You just don't care at all about me, do you?

Woman: "I'm sorry."

Man: "I mean if you cared, would you wear this thing? Wouldn't you fix yourself up a bit? You're falling apart! It's a good thing you have me to put up with you. I mean, I've tried to be patient, OK?"

Woman (her internal monologue): "Why am I so stupid? Why can't I ever get it just right? I need to try harder, because if I lose this guy, well, nobody else is going to want somebody like me."

Sometimes the most hurtful things of all, are what we say to ourselves.

I'd like to conduct a little experiment, and I'd like you to participate. In fact, I'd like you to find out something important about yourself right now.

I'm going to put you in a variety of situations and give

you two responses—two things you might say to yourself as a result. And I'd like you to choose which response fits you best. Which do you find yourself saying most of the time?

Are you ready? OK, here we go.

1. You pass an acquaintance on the street and say "Hello." This person doesn't seem to notice and walks on by. What's your reaction? (A) Maybe he didn't hear me. (B) I must have done something to offend him.

2. Let's say you're facing a challenging task at work. What's your typical response? (A) I'll do the best I can. (B) I just can't afford to make any mistakes!

3. Someone at work does find a mistake in something you've done and points it out. You react by saying (A) Most of the job is OK; I'll fix the mistake. (B) This whole thing is a mess; I've gotten it all wrong!

4. One of your friends fails to show up at your birthday party—as you expected. How do you react? (A) I wish she'd been able to come. (B) She should have come. She would have been here if she really cared.

As you've looked at these situations, do you find that you tend to make the "A" response more often? Or the "B" response?

If you usually go for "B," then you may have adopted what is called "negative self-talk." You've fallen into the habit of repeating things to yourself that just aren't true.

One of the clearest signs of negative self-talk are the words "always" and "never." People say things such as, "I always foul things up." Or, "I'll never be able to do it right." People also use these words when talking about others. "He always comes late." "She never considers my feelings." These are over-generalizations. We find a dark spot and paint the whole world black. That's what "always" and "never" do.

Negative self-talk also is driven by "should." We hang on tightly to that one. What other people *should* do for us. How they *should* behave. And of course, our expectations are often disappointed.

Negative self-talk hangs out in an all-or-nothing universe. If one thing is wrong, then it's all wrong. One mistake, one error, ruins the whole batch.

There is a reason why the things we say to ourselves are so important. They are very important when it comes to changing unhealthy behavior. In this book, we've been looking at truths that change bad habits. And we've seen that behind those habits, behind those addictions, there is usually brokenness; there is usually a hurt or a pain that we're trying to numb. Well, there is a way that this brokenness keeps us trapped. There is a way it keeps pushing us into destructive behavior. And that way is—negative self-talk. That's how this brokenness expresses itself. That's how it keeps controlling us. Negative self-talk keeps us stuck in bad habits. That's what Christian counselors on the front line have discovered.

Paul Coneff: "A lot of times when we get hurt or wounded by someone else, we can also develop false belief systems about the world. Let's say Dad divorces Mom, and he leaves. The child ends up feeling 'I'm not important because my Dad left.' Well, it wasn't the child's fault, but he begins to develop a false belief system about himself, and then he finds ways to cover up those negative feelings that the false belief system brings."

Scott Davis: "It's amazing how we can talk ourselves into all kinds of emotions and feelings—bad or good—simply by negative or positive self-talk."

Bob Oltoff: "Many of the tapes that we play to ourselves that are negative self-talk are lies, and we need to say, 'Wait a minute; is this the truth or is this not the truth?'"

You can take criminals off the street, change their environment, and give them a chance to find honest work. But often they go back to the same life of crime. In their head, they know it's not best, but they're driven by a belief system that tells them they're helpless, that they just can't make it. They feel defeated, they believe their lives are hopeless. Life on the street has taught them that survival depends on stealing, hustling, selling drugs, or some other illegal activity. That's the lie that keeps them trapped in destructive behavior.

Lies imprison us. In the beginning of the book of Romans, Paul sets out to talk about our basic problem as human beings. Notice what he says. "Because, although they knew God, they did not glorify Him as God, nor were thankful, but became futile in their thoughts, and their foolish hearts were darkened. Professing to be wise, they became fools." (Romans 1:21, 22). People in general, Paul argues, know the truth about God from creation. But they refuse to acknowledge that truth. They buy into a lie. In his day, they bowed down before idols; they gave themselves up to vile passions; they "exchanged the truth of God for the lie" (verse 25).

Lies can imprison us. They can darken our hearts. Many times, we learned lies in our childhood. At times, we learned a distorted picture of reality, growing up. And these lies stay with us. They color our view of the world. These are the things we keep repeating. No lie is more powerful than the one we keep telling ourselves in our heads.

Lies are a way for us to hide from the truth. They are a way for destructive behavior patterns to keep their hold on us. Let's look at a few facts about negative self-talk.

First, it's usually automatic and subtle. You hardly notice it. You don't notice how it affects you. It's just an instinctive reaction. You make a mistake, for example, and think: "I'll never get this right!"

Second, negative self-talk is irrational. It may sound like the truth but it falls apart if it's examined at all. It's simply not true that you mess up *everything*. It's simply not true that one mistake ruins the whole batch. It's simply not true that other people *should* always please you. The only reason these lies persist is that they remain unexamined. They're there in the background. They keep coloring our world, but we don't stop to look at the brush strokes.

Finally, negative self-talk reinforces bad habits. It keeps pushing us. If we're chronically anxious, our negative self-talk keeps us avoiding everything we think is dangerous. We avoid more and more; we become anxious more and more.

Negative self-talk keeps us trapped in unrealistic expectations of others. It can keep us disappointed and depressed. Negative self-talk can keep us trapped in abuse. We keep telling ourselves that we don't deserve any better. We keep telling ourselves that there's no way out. Remember, negative self-talk is how pain expresses itself. It's how pain keeps us trapped.

So, let's look for a solution; let's look for an alternative. Just how do we confront these lies? How do we replace negative self-talk with something else?

Bob Oltoff: "I had a woman come in to my office who

was really suffering from feelings of depression. The more I talked with her, the more I could see that she was really trapped with a lot of feelings that were going on from her past. After we looked into her background a little bit, I set up three chairs—one for her to use as she shared her feelings, another chair for her to use as she looked at what she was saying to herself, and a third chair for her to use as we examined what God's Word says about that. After she shared her feelings, she moved to the chair in which she discussed her negative self-talk. When we looked at the negative things that she was playing back, I asked her, 'Where do these tapes come from?' And she was able to name different people—parents, teachers, friends, from the past—who were the source of these negative ideas. Then she moved to the last chair, and she looked at what God's Word says about these things. 'Is that what God is saying to you?' I asked, referring to her negative self-talk. I could see her eyes just light up as she said, 'No! That isn't what God would say. God would say, "I love you." ' "

Scott Davis: "As I begin to have people talk about some of the negative things they say about themselves, I give them new words to use—words from Scripture. And I give them new affirmations they can use when they get in that same situation, instead of tearing themselves up."

I believe that God's truth is a powerful force for dispelling lies. God's truth isn't just a theory on paper. God's truth is a living principle, a living word. Read what James says: "Of His own will He brought us forth by the word of truth, that we might be a kind of firstfruits of His creatures" (James 1:18). This is talking about the new birth, spiritual transformation. How does God accomplish this miracle? Through the "word of truth." In the beginning God said, "Let there be light" and there was light. He spoke, and creatures came to life. He is the Almighty Creator. Well, He's still creating with His word today, His word of truth. He brings to life a new kind of individual, a "firstfruit" of a new creation. Someone who is born again. Someone who is no longer trapped by the old lies.

Listen to what the Creator can do: "For it is the God who commanded light to shine out of darkness, who has shone in our hearts to give the light of the knowledge of the glory of God in the face of Jesus Christ" (2 Corinthians 4:6).

The same God who created light out of darkness, the same God who caused a blazing sun to appear in a dark sky—this God can shine in our hearts. He can illuminate all those dark crevices. He can flood the hidden lies with truth. It's the truth about how wonderful God is, how gracious He is, how just He is. It's the truth about the Father who cherishes. It's a truth that we can see in the loving face of Jesus Christ.

Yes, we may be plagued by blind spots. Yes, we may struggle with lies learned in childhood. Yes, our first instinct may be to repeat negative self-talk. But God has a resource that can illuminate our hearts. He has a way to make the truth sink in deep. Let's look at what Jesus promised His disciples in John 16. You know, these were men who had plenty of blind spots. They had trouble grasping what the kingdom of heaven was all about. But, this is what Jesus said: " 'I still have many things to say to you, but you cannot bear them now. However, when He, the Spirit of truth, has come, He will guide you into all truth' " (John 16:12, 13).

Wow, what a promise! The Holy Spirit will guide us into all truth. Like the disciples, we may not be able to grasp the "many things" that we need to learn. We may have a hard time changing our perspective. But Jesus promises that we can be guided by the Spirit, step by step, into all the truth we need to know. Yes, the light can indeed shine in our hearts, revealing the face of Jesus Christ.

I believe that's true. And I believe that is one of the primary principles of change. That is what pastors and counselors on the front lines are discovering.

Let me give you one example from my own ministry. I'm convinced that dramatic things do happen when God's light breaks through for people. I'm convinced the positive results that occur in people's lives as a result of God's work far exceed those of conventional secular therapies.

Anna is a woman I recently met when I conducted an evangelistic series in Sao Paulo, Brazil. She believed her life was worthless. She was attractive, intelligent, and outgoing, but extremely depressed. On her 23rd birthday, she decided to take her own life. Before ending it all, she wrote letters to her family, to her close friends, and even a letter to God. Miraculously, at the very time she was writing these letters, the telephone rang. The person calling had dialed a wrong number, but he immediately sensed Anna's distress. He began to gently encourage her and present her with hope. Then he invited her to some meetings I was holding. Anna came, desiring a new life. Anna came, desiring to be healed from her brokenness. She came, longing for that pain and that hurt within to go away.

And she sat spellbound as I talked about how, in Christ, we're valuable; in Christ, we're loved; in Christ, we're accepted; in Christ, we can be made whole. Anna confronted her self-talk. She confronted the lies swirling around in her head. She accepted the truth that in Christ's eyes, she was valuable. The lie that had been trapping her unraveled. It lost its grip.

The truth, of course, was obvious enough. But it had to sink in, in a special way. And the Holy Spirit impressed her with reality. God made that impression real in her mind. He made His light shine in her heart. This was the beginning of healing for Anna.

Christian counselors, pastors, and physicians have documented in case after case the dramatic results when God's truth sinks in. The lie is finally confronted with something more powerful. The lie that gives the pain its power over us fades away in God's light. Friends, we need to make a deliberate effort to tell ourselves the truth, to speak God's truth to ourselves. We need to make a conscious effort to listen to the Spirit's voice.

Paul Coneff: "In Hebrews 8 and 10, God says that He will make a covenant, or agreement, with us, and that He will write His law on our minds and on our hearts. I work with Christians every single week who come in and say, 'I know I'm forgiven, but I don't experience it here.' They're not looking for an emotional feeling, but they don't believe God has forgiven them. In Romans, it says we're to confess with our mouth and to believe in our hearts. During this prayer process, Jesus is touching people's minds and their hearts. They already have the knowledge, but they haven't experienced forgiveness yet. And so when they have this experience, then they're able to believe in their heart and confess with their mouth. I'm seeing people set free, because they're experiencing the power of God's Word, touching not just their minds, but their hearts."

No lie is stronger than the one we tell ourselves. And no truth is stronger than the one God helps to sink into our hearts. That enables us to practice positive self-talk. And that can be wonderfully freeing.

Man: "I was waiting, like, ten minutes! What is the matter with you? I think you missed the exit on purpose. You must be trying to humiliate me. What do you think I looked like standing there like an idiot?"

Woman: (her internal monologue:) "Actually, I'm not trying to do anything to you. But you seem to be trying to humiliate me. And I don't deserve that."

Man: "I've tried to be patient, OK. I'm doing the best I can here. But you're always trying to upset me."

Woman: "Listen, I'm sorry that I was a bit late. I'm going to go to the ladies' room now, and you try to get yourself together. When I come back, if you would like to apologize for putting me down, that's fine. If not, then I'm going to go home."

Telling ourselves the truth can prevent others from imposing their lies on us.

Now, let's look at something very important about the truth that God wants to sink into our own hearts. There's one truth that replaces lies more than any other. There's one truth that sheds more light than any other. There's one thing that God wants us to speak more than any other. In Ephesians 4 Paul is talking about lies that trap people. He's talking about the trickery of men, of those deceived by one lie after another. And then he gives this alternative: "Instead, speaking the truth in love, we will in all things grow up into him who is the Head, that is, Christ. From him the whole body . . . grows and builds itself up in love" (Ephesians 4:15, 16, NIV).

How do we grow up into Christ? By speaking the truth in love. How does the body of Christ grow and build itself up? By following the way of love.

Deane Wolcott: "I do believe that the most powerfully transcendent experience of love for most people is the experience of being loved by God. Because that love truly is unconditional, and there are very few times in life when we otherwise experience unconditional love."

Friends, God's truth can be summarized in just one word. *Love.* God's truth is love. God Himself is love. The truth that needs to be poured into darkened hearts is the truth about love. You sense that in these words from the apostle Peter: "Since you have purified your souls in obeying the truth through the Spirit in sincere love of the brethren, love one another fervently with a pure heart" (1 Peter 1:22). Following the truth is intertwined with sincere love, fervent love from a pure heart.

We see the same connection in the writings of the apostle Paul. Notice what he says—it is really a prayer for believers. "I pray that out of his glorious riches he [God] may strengthen you with power through his Spirit in your inner being, so that Christ may dwell in your hearts through faith. And I pray that you, being rooted and established in love, may have power . . . to grasp . . . the love of Christ . . .that surpasses knowledge" (Ephesians 3:16-19, NIV).

We need to be rooted and established in love. We need

to know the love of Christ. That's the truth that needs to strengthen us. That's the truth that needs to illuminate the "inner being" of our hearts. God's love dispels the darkest lies. God's love stamps out shame. How can we be ashamed, how can we feel worthless, when we're cherished by this perfect Father in heaven?

God's love breaks up perfectionism and judgmentalism. And God's love frees us from the prison of our own rebellious choices. The harshest critic can't keep on haranguing you in the face of unconditional acceptance. God's love overturns our false expectations. We learn to give other people a break—because we have been forgiven so graciously. God's love covers all the lies. It fills our hearts with something so much better.

Is God's love deep in your heart today? Or are those lies still running through your own head? Is God's truth shining bright inside? Or are you trapped by negative self-talk?

Isn't it time to give God's perspective a chance? Isn't it time to get rooted and established in love? Please allow the Holy Spirit to lead you into all the truth you need to know. Please allow God to help you start speaking the truth to yourself. Please allow His Word to make you part of a new creation. Please allow God, through His Spirit, to enter into your life and to reveal within the fabric of your being, deep within the inner recesses of your soul, that you're valued, that you're loved, that you're cherished by the Creator of the universe.

Put God in Charge

Behind the habits that trip you up, behind the unhealthy behavior that you just can't shake, behind the emotions that keep you trapped, one question looms very large, one question determines the ultimate outcome: Who's on the throne in your life; who's in control?

It's a question that, one way or another, all of us have to answer.

Karl thought it was his duty to check on what his wife wore every day. He had to be in charge of her wardrobe. He said it was because he didn't want other men looking. But he also had to keep track of what she did every minute during the day. She had to phone him every time she wanted to leave the house.

Karl had to be in charge, he thought, as head of the household. He'd succeeded in controlling his wife very well. But what Karl couldn't control was the rage inside him, the fear inside him, the emptiness inside him. These dark emotions always threatened to overwhelm him.

Myra felt a tremendous need to determine the color of the new carpet in the church and the design of the new pews. She made long appeals at church board meetings.

She lobbied and badgered. She criticized those with different tastes. Myra thought it her duty to have the final say in the exact order of the worship and the type of instruments that should be or shouldn't be used in the service. She thought she needed to correct a lot of errors and set things straight.

What she couldn't set straight were her three adolescent kids at home. They were running wild. They couldn't wait to be free of their mother's ever-watchful eye. They couldn't wait to get into as much mischief as possible.

It's a fact that counselors run into over and over. In their attempts to help people sort out issues on the inside, they find people trying to straighten out stuff on the outside. Individuals who've lost control of their own emotions are desperately trying to control the behavior of others.

In this book, we've been looking at truths that break bad habits. We've been examining fundamental principles, dynamic principles, from the Bible that make positive change possible. We've talked about the necessity of being honest about our situation. We've talked about facing the pain behind our addictions.We've talked about dealing with negative self-talk.

In this chapter, we're going to talk about the last big obstacle to growth. It's the matter of who is in control. And, in a way, it's the bottom line.

Pastors and Christian counselors have discovered that human nature instinctively puts up a lot of defenses. The heart has countless ways of avoiding the hard truth. And one of the ways that people avoid facing the fact that something inside them is out of control is to try to control others. They try to influence feelings on the inside by manipulating behavior on the outside. People who always have to manipulate or control individuals and situations present a difficult challenge.

Deane Wolcott: "For most people, the underlying belief is, 'I have to be strong.' And the way that we demonstrate that we are strong is by maintaining control, keeping our feelings inside, not sharing. It's kind of the military model, you know. You never show you're afraid. But the reality is, that you carry your burdens alone as a result."

Bob Oltoff: "There was a young lady who experienced seeing her father take his life. She was right there when her father pulled the trigger, and she saw it all happen. The result was that she became very obsessive-compulsive in attempting to control every area of her life. Once she got married, she started controlling her husband's life and her children's lives. What was motivating her to act like that? The fear of the pain that would come if she didn't stay in control."

In the New Testament, the Pharisees are a classic example of a group that felt compelled to control others. They were like white-washed tombs, as Jesus pointed out—full of dead men's bones on the inside, but making a fine appearance of piety on the outside. They might be dying inside, but they could observe the letter of the ceremonial law with a great show of phylacteries on their foreheads and ornate, flowing robes.

Jesus saw through all this very quickly. He warned them, " 'You are those who justify yourselves before men, but God knows your hearts' " (Luke 16:15). These were people who, as Paul said, "Glory in appearance, and not in heart" (2 Corinthians 5:12, KJV). And these were people who manipulated others in order to try to cover their own inadequacies. Speaking of their attempts to enforce all kinds of rules and regulations, Jesus made this observation: " 'They bind heavy burdens, hard to bear, and lay them on men's shoulders; but they themselves will not move them with one of their fingers' " (Matthew 23:4).

People control the outside in order to cover up what's lacking on the inside. People who are compelled to control are usually covering up a great deal of emptiness inside.

Scott Davis: "I think that what drives controlling people at the very basic level, is fear. I think there is a lack of self-esteem. The only way such individuals can feel good about themselves is to be in control. If they're controlling all the circumstances and situations around them, then they don't really have to react or respond or deal with the feelings of others. It's also a way to keep people away and not deal with what's truly going on inside them."

Is there a solution for people who have to be in charge in these unhealthy ways? Is there an answer? Christian counselors are starting to make breakthroughs.

Paul Coneff: "If they are praying and they're convicted to give up the anger—because that's what they've been using to protect themselves—then we lead them through a prayer of surrendering to God their need to be in control, their need to be angry in order to feel safe, to protect themselves. We teach them to not say, 'Lord, help

me get over my anger.' Instead, we encourage them to
say, 'Lord if You don't take it from me, if You don't release me from my anger, I will never be released from it.'
The key is coming to the point of being totally 100 per-
cent dependent on God and allowing Him to do what only
He can do. When we are able to get behind that coping
skill, then we're able to move through the pain, through
the lie, and help them to experience freedom."

David Smith: "Sometimes I have found myself being
really angry at somebody—someone who, unfortunately,
wasn't likely to be getting out of my life anytime soon.
That person was right there in my life, and I was totally
incapable of dealing with him or my feelings about him.
I couldn't get past the anger, the desire for revenge, or
the endless rehearsals of the speeches I'd like to make,
but never did. I had the speeches down to perfection. But
all this is a vicious cycle that you just cannot resolve as a
human being. The only thing that does work at all—and
it's a life-long process to make even that work—is to give
the whole scenario to Jesus and say, 'I don't have the
wisdom to handle this. I can't get revenge; I shouldn't
get revenge. I simply want to give this whole situation to
You and allow You to take care of this person and me. I
want You simply to take this out of my life and take the
responsibility for it.' That does set you free. But the next
day you have to set yourself free again with God's help.
That's the only way I have been able to deal with certain
angers that, from a human point of view, were just not
going to be fixed in my own strength."

I believe that people who have to control have to do
one important thing. They have to run into someone who

is bigger, someone who is really in control. They have to run into someone who is bigger and kinder. Controllers are terribly concerned with appearances; they're terribly concerned with how they look. They want others to respect them. They want to occupy the best seat in the house. But Jesus gives us this warning, " 'Whoever exalts himself will be humbled , and he who humbles himself will be exalted' " (Matthew 23:12). You can't pull yourself up to a high position by your own bootstraps. You'll be exposed eventually. You'll be knocked down. It's only when you give up trying that you'll find yourself exalted.

James emphasizes the same principle in his epistle. After urging believers to submit their lives to God, he says: "Humble yourselves in the sight of the Lord, and He will lift you up" (James 4:10). The apostle Peter underlines this truth as well. He writes: "Clothe yourselves with humility toward one another, because, 'God opposes the proud but gives grace to the humble.' Humble yourselves, therefore, under God's mighty hand, that he may lift you up in due time" (1 Peter 5:5, 6, NIV).

When we try to exalt ourselves, we're just setting ourselves up for a fall. We set up our own egos on some kind of a throne. But they don't really belong there. They don't fit. They're always in danger of falling over. And we constantly have to prop them up. God is the One who belongs on the throne of our lives. God is the One, the only One, who deserves to be in charge. And we can find *our* rightful place only by putting Him in charge of our lives.

Peter amplifies this principle. He says, "Sanctify the Lord God in your hearts" (1 Peter 3:15). In other words, "Set apart Christ as Lord in your heart."

That is what has to happen. Christ has got to be in your heart. That's the only way to begin dealing with what's on the inside. That's the only way to begin straightening out your own emotions. That's the only way to begin gaining control of your own life.

Letting God have control. That's essential. If we don't have that, we'll just go on trying to straighten out and control and manipulate things on the outside. And that dooms us to failure.

David Coe: "The first step of the process is the realization of what you're actually doing. Once you realize what you're doing, then you can ask the Lord to come in and fill your heart and start to make those changes. I couldn't make those changes on my own. There's no human way possible for me to change because of the heavy rut that I was really in."

Kim Delaura: "When my husband made the choice to go outside of the marriage and have an affair, it left me feeling very out of control. And in a way that was a good thing for me, because I think this was the one time I saw I couldn't meet the needs of everyone around me. There was nothing I could do to make him act in a different way. It caused me to look upward, to look at Someone bigger than I was, to look at God. I realized that I needed to turn the whole thing—my husband's actions, my emotions, everything—over to God and allow Him to begin working in the way that He chose. I'm not trying now to manipulate or work something different in my life; I'm letting Him take charge of that."

Let me tell you about a man who must have had a very hard time putting God on the throne. His name was Nebuchadnezzar. He presided over the glorious city of

Babylon as the head of a vast empire. He was the most powerful monarch of his day. He controlled the fates of countless people. His story is told in Daniel, chapter 4. Nebuchadnezzar had a huge ego, and he had plenty of resources to feed it. One day, that ego caught up with him. It sort of collapsed in on itself.

He was walking around the roof of his royal palace, surveying the wondrous city that he had rebuilt. And he boasted, "Is not this great Babylon, that I have built for a royal dwelling by my mighty power and for the honor of my majesty?"

Well, shortly after this, Nebuchadnezzar had what we might call a psychotic episode. He just fell apart. He started wandering around with the animals in the fields, eating grass like a cow. His hair grew long, tangled, and dirty. His nails began to look like bird claws. The situation looked hopeless. The Bible speaks about the judgments of God that fell upon Nebuchadnezzar because of his rebellion and his disobedience. All the insecurities, all the unsettling emotions inside this king, had finally overwhelmed him. He could control a vast empire, but he couldn't control the painful emptiness inside.

However, in this dark hour, the prophet Daniel gave a promise that offered hope. He made a prediction. Daniel 4:26 describes this issue of the battle for the throne. At one time, Nebuchadnezzar ruled the throne of his own heart. But now the Bible speaks this wonderful promise: " 'Your kingdom shall be assured to you, after you come to know that Heaven rules' " (Daniel 4:26). The prophet was saying that Nebuchadnezzar could still get his act together if he woke up to the fact of who is really in charge. If he acknowledged who was really supposed to be on the throne.

One day, this powerful monarch did just that. The testimony of Nebuchadnezzar himself is recorded in Daniel. He says that he finally lifted up his eyes to heaven, and his understanding returned to him. This is how he put it: "I blessed the Most High and praised and honored Him who lives forever. At the same time my reason returned to me, . . . I was restored to my kingdom" (Daniel 4:34, 36).

How did Nebuchadnezzar's reason return? How did he recover from his total collapse? By blessing the Most High. By honoring Him who lives forever. By putting the rightful Person on the throne. That's how this man occupied his rightful place again. And that's the only way that you and I can have a properly balanced life.

Friends, we can't control enough things to control what's happening inside us. It just doesn't work. If Nebuchadnezzar couldn't do it—with all the resources at his disposal—no one can. Only God can take care of what's happening deep inside us. And He can only do so if He's occupying the throne of our lives. It's only when we submit to Him, when we humble ourselves before Him, that we will find peace and be exalted. God in control is how we gain control. It's the essential final step in dealing with habits that bind us, behaviors that keep us trapped.

Scott Davis: "The whole issue of having to be in control centers around fear. As we understand God and allow Him to embrace us—and as we embrace Him—He begins to replace that fear with His perfect love. We no longer fear the judgment. So we no longer need to be in control."

Deane Wolcott: "If you genuinely believe that God is looking for a relationship with each one of us and that He values us as being uniquely special—in fact, that He values us so much that each one of us is worth the life of His Son—then it's very easy to turn over control to a God like that. It all comes down to your fundamental view of God and His character."

Who's on the throne of your life today? Who's the boss? Are you occupying a place that really belongs to God? You will never really be in control of your life as long as you're trying to control everything. Remember that you will never really be in control of yourself unless you relinquish control to God.

I challenge you to make a big step, a definite step right now. I challenge you to truly submit to Jesus Christ as the Lord of your life. He can be trusted. He's wise enough. He's strong enough. He's caring enough. He can come in and make a big difference in your life. He can write His law in your heart and mind.

So please, give Him a chance. See what He can do. Put Him in charge. Let go of your futile attempts to run everything. God has better plans for you. God has a better place for you. Let's start finding it right now.

The Sabbath Boundary

So much is going on, so much is flying by in our lives, that it's hard to stop. It's hard to recognize boundaries. Sometimes you can't even figure out where you leave off and where everything else begins. You may not know it yet, but God has a suggestion on how we can actually stop the relentless rush of time!

In recent years we have become keenly aware of something called "boundary issues." Some people have a hard time setting boundaries in their lives. Some people have a hard time saying "no" when they should.

Take a woman like Rita, for example. She's a single mother trying hard to raise three little boys. She also has some friends from church who are rather demanding. They expect her to organize social events for the singles group. They expect her to lead out in outreach activities. "This is her gift," they say, "and she ought to be exercising it."

So Rita tries. She badly needs the affirmation of her friends. But she finds herself stretched very thin. Her children require a lot of attention. And there are always so many church events to prepare for. Rita's life is getting out of control, but she just can't say "no." She thinks it's her duty to always say "yes" to her friends.

Then, take a man like Mike. He's an insurance salesman who likes to keep everybody happy. He tries to keep his wife happy. He tries to keep the people at work happy. And he tries to keep his mother happy. She seems to always need him—even though she's in good health. She needs him to fix a leaky faucet or the jammed garbage disposal. She needs him to sort out her bills. She needs him to run errands. She needs him around when she's depressed.

Mike's wife wonders why he's gone all the time. She can't understand why her mother-in-law can't do things for herself. And Mike feels torn. He wants to be a better husband, but how can he say "no" when his mother calls? That would make him feel like an ungrateful son.

Rita and Mike are classic examples of people who can't set good boundaries. They are constantly bending themselves out of shape in order to fit into other people's shapes. And so they lose a shape of their own. They can't keep people away who are too intrusive or too controlling. They can't tell people "no" when they need to. They can't say, "I'm sorry, but that's an unreasonable expectation." They can't say, "I'm sorry, but I can't fit that into my life right now."

People without boundaries take on too much. They are molded by the expectations of others, and so they are forever caught up in a rush of trying to do too much, trying to please too many people. All of us get caught up in that rush in one way or another. In our world today, it's easy to take on too many chores. Everything seems to happen faster and faster. The speed of the microchip doubles every eighteen months! Two-day express mail used to be fast enough for most everybody. But now, we have to have overnight deliveries. And even that is "snail mail," according to people hooked on the instant communication of email.

Even names have to get faster. "Federal Express" just took too long to say, so now those trucks and planes speeding by read: "Fed Ex."

The world keeps going faster, and that makes all the demands placed upon us tougher to deal with. And it makes the struggles of people without boundaries more acute. How do we put up boundaries in a world in which one day just flows into the next, one week into the next, one year into the next? How do we stop the rush in a way that's meaningful for us?

I'd like to suggest that God Himself has given us a good starting point. He has shown us a very meaningful boundary, a boundary in time. Let's take a look at it. We first find it in the book of Genesis. In the first few chapters of Genesis we discover that God, at Creation, gave us two important institutions. The first was marriage. Our Creator united Adam and Eve as one flesh. He gave them the Garden of Eden as a beautiful home in which to raise their family.

The second gift from God is described in the second chapter of Genesis: "Then God blessed the seventh day and sanctified it, because in it He rested from all His work which God had created and made" (Genesis 2:3). At the end of the six days of Creation week, God instituted the Sabbath. He made the seventh day special and holy. He rested from His work. And this became an example for His people. They, too, were to rest from all their work on the Sabbath.

The Sabbath was a holy boundary placed in the weekly

cycle. It stopped the endless flow of time, the endless rush of chores.

The Sabbath is a way to stop. But it means more than just time off from work. The book of Deuteronomy reminds God's people to " 'Observe the Sabbath day by keeping it holy, as the Lord your God has commanded you' " (Deuteronomy 5:12, NIV).

We are advised to keep this certain day holy. It's a day set apart from all the other days of the week. It's special. It's quality time. It's a time for investing in our most important relationships—our relationship with God and our relationships with loved ones.

And, yes, it's a time when we can say "no" to all the other demands, all the other things that clutter up our lives. The Sabbath is a boundary that gives us breathing room.

The Sabbath calls us away from our usual routines. It asks us to make the pursuit of spiritual things a delight. Reading good books, exploring nature, spending quiet time together as a family—these are the things we typically neglect. Why? Because we don't have good boundaries. We let so many other demands fill up our lives.

Now, I want you to understand how unique this Sabbath idea is in the whole history of religion. There are many holy *things* in the religions of the world. People have ascribed holiness to everything from bones of the saints to Brahma cattle. Men have worshiped idols of every conceivable kind. And there are many holy *places* in the religions of the world. Hindus travel thousands of miles to bathe in the sacred waters of the Ganges River. Moslems make long pilgrimages to the holy city of Mecca. Buddhists revere the site where Buddha experienced enlightenment.

But in the Bible, we find the utterly unique idea of holiness in *time*. God created a holy setting in which human beings could be specially blessed, but He did not restrict it to a certain location. We don't have to make long pilgrimages to arrive at God's holy place. No, He has placed His holy setting in time, equally accessible to everyone. It's a quality time for everyone. It's a boundary for everyone.

People without boundaries are carrying too many burdens. They are oppressed by the demands and expectations of others. Did you know that deliverance from oppression is one of the things memorialized by the Sabbath boundary God gives us? The Sabbath symbolizes deliverance.

We've already seen how the Sabbath calls us back to our Creator, the One who rested on the seventh day of Creation, the One who wants to make us healthy and whole. The Sabbath also calls us back to God as our personal Redeemer.

Look at how the book of Deuteronomy amplifies the meaning of the Sabbath. In its restatement of the Ten Commandments we find this: " ' "And remember that you were a slave in the land of Egypt, and that the Lord your God brought you out from there by a mighty hand and by an outstretched arm; therefore the Lord your God commanded you to keep the Sabbath day" ' " (Deuteronomy 5:15). The Sabbath, you see, is a memorial of God's deliverance. He is the great Rescuer. And whom did He rescue? People who had to work all the time. Slaves in Egypt toiling through the monotonous hours. Slaves with no hope that their endless labor would ever give them freedom. That's who God rescued. His mighty hand and outstretched arm swept them from under the control of a tyrannical Pharaoh.

There are many slaves today who need a similar rescue. Their endless toil serves to make them only less and less free; they have less and less time. Their endless attempts to please everybody make them only more frustrated. Their endless attempts to meet everyone's demands make them only more hopeless. And there is no tyrant as merciless as our own desperate fear, our own sense of inadequacy. We need God the Deliverer today just as much as the Hebrews did. We need Him to come in and give us His Sabbath, His boundary, at the end of our week.

He says, "Stop! There is only one way to be free—and that is to trust your Creator. Yes, trust Me. Invest your time in a relationship with Me, and I will become your Deliverer."

Thank God for Sabbath rest. It's the answer for our stress-intensive environment. It's a meaningful boundary for us. It tells us there is more to life than just a wearying routine.

It seems that people with boundary problems often grew up in homes where the boundaries were blurred. They constantly had to try to please someone in order to be accepted. Perhaps as a child they even had to take care of an addicted or needy parent. They may have learned to take on other people's problems as their own. In other words, people with boundary problems often have acceptance problems. They keep working so hard in order to be accepted. They can't rest because they never feel quite accepted.

Well, let me share with you what the New Testament has to say about Sabbath rest and why that rest is relevant to us as believers. The Sabbath actually shows us that we can truly rest in Christ. That's right—rest in Christ.

The writer of the book of Hebrews makes this clear. He writes about the seventh day, pointing out what this day of rest really means for believers. This is what he says: "There remains therefore a rest for the people of God. For he who has entered His [God's] rest has himself also ceased from his works as God did from His" (Hebrews 4:9, 10).

Entering into Sabbath rest means that we stop depending on our works; we no longer try to manufacture salvation; we no longer try to be accepted on the basis of our own good works. God has done the work for us in Christ. Christ has completed the work of our redemption.

He did it by the shores of the Sea of Galilee. He did it on the dusty trails of Judea. He did it in the streets of Jerusalem. Jesus Christ lived out a perfect, righteous life in *our* world, in *our* environment. And then He poured out that life on the cross—deliberately, willingly. He gave up His perfect life as a substitute for our sinful life.

In a sense, this Carpenter from Nazareth carved out a special dwelling for us fashioned from His righteousness. We can find refuge there; we can be safe there. His work is complete. It is finished. We can rest confidently in the forgiveness that Christ offers. We can know that, *in Christ*, we are accepted by the heavenly Father.

Sabbath rest is about being accepted by our Father in heaven. Do you see why this can be so meaningful for people without boundaries? The Sabbath boundary says, "Here is where you can stop; here is where you can rest. You can say "no" to demanding people because God has said "yes" to you. He has said "yes" in Jesus

Christ. He has given you righteousness in Jesus Christ.

The Sabbath is a meaningful boundary that can stick with you. It can stick with you in a world of constant change and widespread confusion. It can be an island of stability.

Our families need that today. Our children need that so much today. All around them things are falling apart. Traditional values are crumbling; families are fractured; trust is betrayed. But the Sabbath proclaims that God is constant; His values are unchanging.

Look at these words of God found in Exodus: " ' "You shall surely observe My sabbaths; for *this* is a sign between Me and you throughout your generations, that you may know that I am the Lord who sanctifies you" ' " (Exodus 31:13, NASB).

The Sabbath is a sign that continues through generation after generation. It points generation after generation toward the Lord who sanctifies us, who sets us apart. Its observance can mark out a boundary between what is truly important and what is not so important. It can help us concentrate on the things that matter most.

I'd like you to look at some very interesting words in the book of Isaiah. Here the prophet is asking his people to rebuild their faith. He's calling them back to spiritual values. This is what he says: "Those from among you shall build the old waste places; you shall raise up the foundations of many generations; and you shall be called the Repairer of the Breach, the Restorer of Streets to Dwell In. 'If you turn away your foot from the Sabbath, from doing your pleasure on My holy day, and call the Sabbath a delight, the holy day of the Lord honorable, . . . I will cause you to ride on the high hills of the earth' " (Isaiah 58:12-14).

Those who rebuild the faith are called Repairers of the Breach. Obviously, there was a breach in the protective wall that surrounded God's people. That boundary had been broken down. And Isaiah's call to repair the breach is associated with a call to restore the Sabbath, to make it a delight again, to make it honorable again.

Why? Because the Sabbath is a meaningful boundary. It's part of that protective wall—part of God's circle of care—around us. He wants us to be able to say "no" as well as "yes." He wants us to have a shape, a meaningful identity. He wants to give us a space in which to grow.

I'm thankful that God is our Creator. He wants to make us whole. I'm thankful that God is our Redeemer. He wants to deliver us from our burdens. I'm thankful that we can truly rest in Jesus Christ. I'm thankful that He can make us Repairers of the Breach. We can draw meaningful boundaries. We can be free. We can ride on the high hills of the earth.

A story is told of that terrible time when countless people were sent to Nazi concentration camps. At the train terminal in one of the death camps, the SS officers began separating able-bodied men from the women and children.

One father there was a member of a royal family. He realized with a start that he might never see his young son again. So he knelt down beside the boy and held him by the shoulders. "Michael," he said. "No matter what happens, I want you to always remember one thing. You're special; you're the son of a king."

Soon, father and son were separated by the soldiers. They were marched off to different sections of the camp. The two never saw each other again.

Michael learned much later that his father had perished in a gas chamber. And he had to go out alone and try to make his way in the world. But his father's last words would always stay with him. "You're the son of a king." Michael determined that, whatever came, he would behave like the son of a king.

The Sabbath is an important message from our heavenly Father, a sign that declares: "You are a child of the King of the universe. I claim you as my own."

And it's a sign that we can always carry with us—a reminder of our special identity. You don't have to be pressured to fit into someone else's mold. You don't have to be manipulated into conforming to someone else's shape. God is shaping you as His child. God is claiming you as His own. He wants you to know that you are a child of the King.

Do you need to draw a meaningful boundary in your life today? Do you need to have quality time with your Maker, your Redeemer? Do you need to truly rest in Jesus Christ?

I invite you to make the Sabbath experience a part of your walk with God. I invite you to stop the endless rush of time, the endless demands, the endless chores. I invite you to begin experiencing Sabbath rest.

Make that decision now.

FREE
Bible
Reading
Guides

Call toll free
1-800-253-3000
or mail the
coupon below
Today!

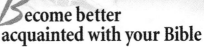

*B*ecome better
acquainted with your Bible

- *No cost now or in the future.*
- *Designed especially for
  busy people like you.*
- *Study at home.*
- *These guides will bring
  the Bible to life.*

☐ **Yes!** Please send me the
26 **FREE** Bible Reading Guides.

Name _____

Address _____

City _____

State/Province _____ Postal Code _____

*Please mail this
completed coupon to:* **DISCOVER**

 it is written • Box O • Thousand Oaks, CA 91360